SPIRITLED WOMAN BIBLE STUDY:
DEBORAH

Dr. Fuchsia Pickett

Charisma®
HOUSE
Books about Spirit-Led Living

SPIRITLED WOMAN BIBLE STUDY: DEBORAH by Fuchsia Pickett
Published by Charisma House
A part of Strang Communications Company
600 Rinehart Road
Lake Mary, Florida 32746
www.charismahouse.com

Unless otherwise noted, all Scripture quotations are from the
King James Version of the Bible.

Scripture quotations marked AMP are from the Amplified Bible.
Old Testament copyright © 1965, 1987 by the Zondervan
Corporation. The Amplified New Testament copyright © 1954,
1958, 1987 by the Lockman Foundation. Used by permission.

Scripture quotations marked NAS are from the New American
Standard Bible. Copyright © 1960, 1962, 1963, 1968, 1971,
1972, 1973, 1975, 1977 by the Lockman Foundation. Used by
permission.

Scripture quotations marked NIV are from the Holy Bible, New
International Version. Copyright © 1973, 1978, 1984,
International Bible Society. Used by permission.

Library of Congress Catalog Card Number: 98-94938
International Standard Book Number: 0-88419-586-4

02 03 04 05   7 6 5 4 3
Printed in the United States of America

Contents

Introduction

Welcome to The SpiritLed Woman Bible Study Series. In this study guide we will be looking at one of the Bible's most courageous women—Deborah, prophet and judge of Israel during a twenty-year period of captivity by the Canaanites. In this fascinating historical account we learn how one woman who obeyed the Spirit of God not only led a nation but actually became a deliverer for the people of God.

The role of women in leadership is probably one of the most controversial issues in the church today. Can women be leaders? Can they hold positions of authority over men? The life of Deborah, as recorded in the fourth chapter of the Book of Judges, stands as an undeniable proof of the unique position of leadership this prophetess and judge in Israel—and forerunner for all Christian women from that time forward—fulfilled as she moved forward in her divine destiny on earth.

Who was Deborah? What significance does her life

reveal for women today? How does she teach us the ways of God in His dealings with mankind? The Book of Judges records the life of Deborah in enough detail for us to learn the answers to these questions and much more.

The theme of this Bible study on Deborah, God's woman in Israel, is "ingathering of the spoil." We will see how God supernaturally spoke to Deborah, led her into a divinely ordained partnership with Barak, and assisted this team in defeating their enemies and inheriting the spoils from the enemy.

As you study may you also move forward into your destiny. Perhaps God has a divinely ordained partnership awaiting you. As you develop the characteristics of Deborah within your life, like Barak, your partner in ministry may face God's challenge of ministry with the declaration: "If you go with me, I will go; but if you don't go with me, I won't go" (Judg. 4:8, NIV).

Objectives of This Bible Study

The SpiritLed Woman Bible Study Series contains three study guides, each twelve chapters long. It is designed to inspire women to study the Bible—alone or in groups. These booklets are ideal for group study and, at twelve chapters each, would work well as quarterly studies. With the addition of Fuchsia Pickett's *How to Search the Scriptures*—an in-depth book that teaches how to study and interpret the Word of God—as an additional study book, an entire year of study could be accomplished. The series includes study booklets on *Esther,* a study guide covering the historical importance of this brave woman's call "for such a time as this"; *Ruth*, a study guide relating the glorious love story of a woman called to the lineage of Christ; and *Deborah*, this study that you are about to begin.

The goals for this study of Deborah are:

- To introduce you to Deborah, forerunner of God's pattern for Christian women in the church.
- To take a close look at the controversial issue of women in leadership and apply biblical concepts and principles to help resolve this issue.
- To recognize the power of the Holy Spirit to prepare and equip women in prophetic ministry.
- To provide a pattern for Christian women for administering godly justice in the situations and circumstances of their lives and those of their family and friends.
- To show the supernatural power of God to lead us into victory over our enemies, bestowing upon us the "spoils" of the enemy as our spiritual inheritance.

To complete this study, you will want to have available for use a King James Version of the Bible. You may also find it helpful to use another Bible translation and a Bible dictionary or concordance as you study.

As you proceed with this study, may the revelations contained in the look at Deborah, a forerunner for all Christian women, change your life and your understanding of your own unique divine destiny in this world.

1

A Forerunner in History

Deborah stands as a forerunner for all Christian women in the church today. The dictionary defines a *forerunner* as "one that precedes and indicates the approach of another." By looking at the life of Deborah, Christian women today can move forward in their own divine destinies by following the principles and patterns evidenced by this mighty woman of God. Like a skier who is commissioned to run the downhill course of an Olympic competition before the start of a race between Olympic challengers, Deborah shows us the course of godly womanhood laid out by God, including our role and position as women in partnership with men.

Prophet and Judge

Deborah is the first of two people in the Bible who were officially considered to be both *judge* and *prophet*. The other was Samuel, who was called by

God to be first prophet and then judge. (See 1 Samuel 3:1–20 and 1 Samuel 7.) In addition to Deborah and Samuel, both Moses and Joshua also operated in this dual capacity of prophet and judge.

By the time Deborah is introduced in the pages of biblical history, she has already received her calling from God as both prophet and judge. But we can learn much about these special "mantles of ministry" from the record of Samuel's call.

Distinctions for the call to prophet

- A prophet(ess) is called to provide access to the word of God in a place where there is a need for God's word and direction to be given.

  And the child Samuel ministered unto the LORD before Eli. And the word of the LORD was precious [rare] in those days; there was no open vision.

  —1 SAMUEL 3:1

- A prophet(ess) receives direct communication from God.

  And the LORD called Samuel again the third time. And he arose and went to Eli, and said, Here am I; for thou didst call me. And Eli perceived that the LORD had called the child. Therefore Eli said unto Samuel, Go, lie down: and it shall be, if he call thee, that thou shalt say, Speak, LORD; for thy servant heareth.

  —VERSES 8–9

- A prophet(ess) receives information about

future, as well as present, actions of God.
Often the information about future events
will be presented to the prophet(ess) from
God as the consequence or reward of present
actions by believers.

And the LORD said to Samuel, Behold, I will do
a thing in Israel, at which both the ears of every
one that heareth it shall tingle. In that day I will
perform against Eli all things which I have
spoken concerning his house: when I begin, I
will also make an end. For I have told him that
I will judge his house for ever for the iniquity
which he knoweth; because his sons made
themselves vile, and he restrained them not.
And therefore I have sworn unto the house of
Eli, that the iniquity of Eli's house shall not be
purged with sacrifice nor offering for ever.
—VERSES 11–14

* The prophet(ess) recognizes the fearful responsibility (s)he has been given to share
  the message from God.

And Samuel lay until the morning, and opened
the doors of the house of the LORD. And Samuel
feared to shew Eli the vision.
—VERSE 15

* As the prophet(ess) is faithful to deliver *all* the
  words of the Lord, the Lord "grows" that person
  into greater roles of responsibility and blessing.

And Samuel grew, and the LORD was with him,

and did let none of his words fall to the ground.

—VERSE 19

Q: Consider the above distinctives of the role of prophet or prophetess. Describe a time in your own life when God spoke to your heart, giving you a clear vision or word about a situation in your own life or in the life of another person, helping you to understand not only what was presently happening, but also giving you a word about what should be done to remedy the situation.

_____

_____

_____

_____

Q: Were you able to help another person understand his or her personal situation through this word you received from God? How?

_____

_____

_____

_____

> *Q: Did you recognize the prophetic voice of God in this situation?*

_____

_____

_____

_____

_____

_____

_____

_____

Deborah was the third woman prophet. Rachel was the first, and Miriam was the second.

Distinctions of the call to judge

Deborah was also the third judge in Israel. The role of judge was a divinely appointed role, and this can be seen in the biblical account of the call of the first two judges. Caleb's nephew, Othniel, was the first. Of his call to judge, the Bible records:

> The spirit of the LORD came upon him, and he judged Israel, and went out to war.
> —JUDGES 3:10

The second judge was Ehud; he was known as the "left-handed judge" who overcame the Moabites.

Q: Think about your own life. Has there been a time when the Lord has given you discernment regarding a situation that required your rendering justice or advising another of God's word of judgment? Describe this experience.

_____

_____

_____

_____

_____

_____

_____

As in the role of prophet, the role of judge was initiated by God because of a vacuum of righteousness among the Israelites.

> In those days there was no king in Israel, but every man did that which was right in his own eyes.
>   —JUDGES 17:6; CF. 18:1; 19:25

This verse, repeated over and over in the Book of Judges, gives the keynote of the whole time of the judges as shown in the Book of Judges. The function of the judges of Israel not only included the administering of the law and rites of the Lord, but also that of

delivering the Israelites from the power of their enemies, much as would be expected of a king.

The number *three* represents completeness. So
Deborah's life, as the third, provides a spiritual picture
of the completeness of her work as both prophet and
judge in Israel at this time. When Deborah emerges
in the fourth chapter of Judges, Israel is again in a
time of disobedience. The people had done evil in
the sight of the Lord, and He sold them into bondage
at the hand of Jabin, king of Canaan.

Deborah was used to deliver Israel from the second
longest captivity in the Book of Judges—a twenty-
year captivity. The longest period of captivity lasted
forty years, and it ended with Samson's heroic act of
deliverance.

The age of the judges ended when Samuel
anointed Saul as the first king of Israel. Today Christ
stands as our King of kings and Lord of lords. The
Holy Spirit has been sent as the "voice" of God, and
Christ's great act of deliverance at Calvary has given
every believer the right to have a personal, intimate
relationship with our King. Yet, as in the days of
Deborah, disobedience still rules in the hearts of
many people.

As we take a closer look at this forerunner, may
each of us desire to follow her course of righteousness so our lives can shine as a clear beacon. Our
world needs to be able to hear the voice of God
clearly and specifically giving fresh revelation for
every circumstance of life. Our world needs
Deborahs who will lead the nations into deliverance.
We have a enemy that must be conquered and an inheritance that must be snatched from the enemies'
camp.

Q: What situation are you or your family facing where a clear, prophetic revelation of God's will would bring a long-awaited solution?

_____

_____

_____

Q: For what circumstance in your life do you need a supernatural, God-ordained deliverance?

_____

_____

_____

Q: Write a prayer asking God to speak clearly to you, giving you His revelation and direction to overcome your captivity to the enemies' bondage. Remember to repent of any acts of disobedience that could be hindering God's supernatural deliverance.

_____

_____

_____

2

An Inheritance of Fruitfulness

Deborah governed as judge over Israel in spite of a twenty-year captivity to the Canaanites. Day after day she administered justice and settled disputes. The name *Deborah* means "bee." It is characteristic of her systematic, orderly style of government. She was the one who knew where to go to gather the honey of God's word. In her prophetic role she demonstrated the orderliness of a God-directed life. She responded to God through discipline, and she encouraged the Israelites to do the same. In her governmental role as judge, she demonstrated her astute discernment and perception.

> *Q: Where in your life do you need to demonstrate God-directed orderliness?*

_____

_____

_____

_____

> *Q: Where do you need to be more disciplined?*

_____

_____

_____

_____

> *Q: For what situations do you need to develop more discernment and perception?*

_____

_____

_____

_____

There were two Deborahs in the Bible—our Deborah of Judges 4–5 and Rebekah's nurse.

Whenever you come across a biblical record of

two people (and two only) who carry the same name, learn to see the spiritual picture their name produces. Let's take a look at the other Deborah.

> But Deborah Rebekah's nurse died, and she was buried beneath Bethel under an oak: and the name of it was called Allonbachuth.
>
> —GENESIS 35:8

This nurse, who had been drawn out of the world, cared for Jacob and Esau. She had the job of protecting, nurturing, caring for, and being a companion to Israel in its beginning stages, because she was nursemaid to Jacob (whose name was changed to *Israel*). She cared for Israel in his beginning as a person. She outlived Rebekah.

The spiritual picture of Deborah as protector, nurturer, and companion is enlarged as we look now at our Deborah of Judges 4. Deborah the judge was married to Lapidoth, whose name means "light; to shine forth." Deborah was a married woman as well as being a judge of the people of Israel. That shocks some people, because they think when you get married you can't ever do anything for God. They say, "But I am married." So am I, and I was a mother when I was called to preach. We don't set our times or tell God who we are—He knows who we are.

Perhaps in your own life you have fulfilled the role of the first Deborah by nurturing or caring for some person or something in its beginnings. As mothers we do this. When we walk with someone through the beginning days of conversion, encouraging and discipling them, we fulfill this role. When you work in the inception stages of ministry you are filling this role.

11

But the characteristics of the other Deborah—
Deborah the prophetess and judge—need to be
developed in our lives as well. You may need to
expand your vision of your destiny to do this. You may
need to stand for God in the midst of adversity or
testing to fulfill this role. But through this forerunner
God has called each of us to a higher plane, a deeper
walk, a fuller revelation of our place in the church.

> *Q:* How have you fulfilled the function of pro-
> tector, nurturer, and companion to someone
> or something in its beginnings (example:
> mother, soulwinner, ministry developer, and
> so on)?

> *Q:* How have you learned to move into the
> characteristics of Deborah as prophetess and
> judge?

> *Q: Where do you still need to grow spiritually to be prepared to do this?*

_____

_____

_____

Deborah came from the tribe of Ephraim. Ephraim was the youngest son of Joseph. His name means "to be fruitful." Because Deborah was from the tribe of Ephraim, many pictures of the attributes of a forerunner can be seen in the blessing Moses prayed over Ephraim in Deuteronomy 33:13–17. Just as Ephraim was to produce these characteristics in his life, so too was Deborah as a forerunner for Christian womanhood—and so too must we.

Let's look at each of these characteristics of a forerunner.

- *Rain and dew* symbolize revival and the everyday presence of God in our lives.

> *Q: Are you experiencing revival and a daily awareness of the presence of God in your life? Describe this experience.*

_____

_____

- *Fruitfulness* includes the fruits of the sun (such as grapes) and the yield of the mouth (indicating plentiful grain crops). Another fruit of the sun is olives, from which we get anointing oil. The forerunner is anointed to produce the ability to fully satisfy hunger—capable of giving both bread and wine.

> *Q:* How have you learned to produce the spiritual bread and wine that are so vital to the growing Christian's life?

- *The chief products of the ancient mountains* include fuel, coal, water, goats, lumber, gold, diamonds, copper, bronze, and the precious things of the hills. A forerunner is fully equipped to minister to the diversity of need among the people of the world—and of the church.

> *Q:* How has God enabled you to minister to the diverse needs of people around you? Give two examples.

- *Precious gifts of the earth* include oil, clay, brick, opals, and salt. Even in the rarest of life's resources—and those of the spirit—a forerunner has access to the things that are most costly and yet most capable of providing shelter, sustenance, and security. The oil of anointing, the foundational truths of clay and brick, the security of precious stones, and the sustenance of salt must be produced in the life of a forerunner.

> *Q: Describe a time when you were able to develop one of these precious gifts of earth in your life or impart it to the life of another.*

- *Favor with God* represents the prophetic role of a forerunner.

> *Q: How have you achieved favor with God?*

- *Right of rulership* represents the civil role of a forerunner as she administers justice in her life and the lives of those around her.

> *Q: Do you demonstrate a life of disciplined justice? How are you working to become more disciplined in your spiritual life?*

_____

_____

_____

The spiritual picture of the lives of these two Deborahs demonstrates the characteristics of the woman of God. If we develop these characteristics in our lives, we will be prepared to impact our world and our churches with the prophetic vision of a deliverer. This is our inheritance. Learn to live a life of fruitfulness as a result of this inheritance.

3

Palm Tree Justice

In this chapter we will take a closer look at Deborah's function in Israel as judge. The Israelites during the period of the judges were not a "whole" nation. Each of the twelve tribes from the time of their exodus from Egypt had been assigned specific regions of the Promised Land as their inheritance. Each tribe jealously guarded its own interest, taking little interest in neighboring tribes. The internal discord that erupted in the land was so threatening that it became doubtful that the Israelites could hold on to their God-given land of promise.

Deborah As Judge

In addition to the internal discord, the former inhabitants of the land retained their hold on large tracts of land, looking upon the newcomers as an easy target. Added to these two factors was the devastating influence of idolatry. The people of Israel did evil against Jehovah God, and as a result God allowed them to be sold into slavery at the hand of their enemies.

If—and only when—the Israelites repented of their evil ways and called upon the one true God, then He raised up a deliverer who saved them. They regained their inherited land, and they remained at rest until their repetitive sinning led them into the same cycle again.

Deborah has historically been named "the most courageous of the judges." She ruled during one of the most devastating captivities, yet she ruled successfully for twenty years—in the face of the opposition of the enemy.

> *Q: What does the success of Deborah as a judge during such a critical time of captivity say to you about her character and tenacity?*

_____

_____

_____

> *Q: How can this example from Deborah's life help you in a time of difficulty that you may be facing?*

_____

_____

In Deborah's function as judge, the Israelites "came to her." The word *came* always functions as an action word. It indicates an ascending process.

> And the children of Israel again did evil in the sight of the LORD, when Ehud was dead. And the LORD sold them into the hand of Jabin king of Canaan, that reigned in Hazor; the captain of whose host was Sisera, which dwelt in Harosheth of the Gentiles. And the children of Israel cried unto the LORD: for he had nine hundred chariots of iron; and twenty years he mightily oppressed the children of Israel. And Deborah, a prophetess, the wife of Lapidoth, she judged Israel at that time. And she dwelt under the palm tree of Deborah between Ramah and Bethel in mount Ephraim: and the children of Israel came up to her for judgment.
>
> —JUDGES 4:1–5

A palm tree is a fruitful tree. It is one of the trees of which every part of it can be used—even its seed. The seed of palm trees, loaded with nutrients, is often fed to camels. Thus, even in her choice of "courtrooms" we can see the fulfillment of the prophecy given to the tribe of Ephraim—and thus to Deborah.

She ruled from her palm tree between two towns—Ramah and Bethel. The name *Ramah* means "elevated," and the name *Bethel* means "the house of God." It is significant to note that Samuel, the other person who held the official titles of prophet and judge, came from Ramah, the town near Deborah. Deborah's hometown was named *Beeroth,* meaning "wells."

The names of these three towns help us to recognize an important element of Deborah's reign as judge. An elevated house of God produces wells of judgment and prophetic vision, which, produced together, initiate an ongoing deliverance.

Ramah was located five miles out of Jerusalem. As its name indicates, the countryside surrounding Beeroth is hilly, with the little town located at the top of a hill. Thus we get the spiritual picture that the people had to ascend in order to seek judgment from God's messenger, who judged righteously, seemingly oblivious to the oppression around her.

Think about a time in your personal life when God brought justice (or judgment) to a situation you were facing. Answer the following questions in light of God's justice:

> *Q: How did you recognize your need to go into the "house of God" as a result of God's intervention in this situation?*

_____

_____

> *Q: In what way did the path or steps you had to take to line up with the justice of God in this situation demonstrate your need to "ascend" to a higher spiritual level than the one on which you were presently living?*

_____

_____

> *Q: Did you recognize the "deep wells" of spiritual revelation that God's intervening action in your situation revealed to you? What were these deeper truths of God?*

_____

_____

_____

_____

_____

_____

_____

As judge over Israel, Deborah was leading Israel at that time. She was not the only woman in history to play such a pivotal part in the history of God's chosen people. Esther had been brought to the kingdom "for such a time as this" (Esther 4:14). Ruth had been divinely uprooted from her own people in Moab to fulfill the lineage of our Lord Jesus Christ through the son she bore with Boaz, a type of our Kinsman-Redeemer Christ (Ruth 4:17). And Mary, the mother of Jesus, was commissioned to her glorious role in the fullness of time. (See Galatians 4:4.)

Kathryn Kuhlman, another forerunner for Christian women, once said, "God does not operate by gender, but by the anointing. The anointing breaks the yoke."

> Q: Has your gender inhibited you in your own mind from moving forward in your divine destiny? Explain.

_____

_____

_____

_____

_____

Describe, by answering the following questions, how you have learned to move forward as a forerunner for other women by operating by the anointing—not by gender.

> Q: Like Esther, how have you recognized a calling on your life in a specified area "for such a time as this"?

_____

_____

_____

_____

_____

> *Q:* How has God led you as He led Ruth to a new beginning among a new land and people so that you might be able to "give birth" to a part of the bride of Christ, a new believer in the church?

> *Q:* What glorious role has God commissioned you to fulfill, much as Mary was commissioned, that occurred "in the fulness of time"?

Administering the justice of God is an awesome responsibility. It requires courage, tenacity, discernment, vision, and a willingness to abide in the house of God—elevated above the devastation and despair of the captivity of the enemy that may surround you. Determine that your life will demonstrate the characteristics of Deborah, the courageous third judge of Israel.

> *Q: Write a prayer asking God to give you the determination and wisdom to administer the justice of God in your own life and in the lives of people in your sphere of influence.*

_____

_____

_____

_____

4

An Oppressive Enemy

The idolatry of the Israelites had caused them to lose the divine protection of God and had forced them into the oppression of a cruel Canaanite king. For twenty years they were oppressed by Jabin, until the time God led Deborah into a partnership with Barak. God directed and supernaturally assisted this team to lead the nation of Israel to a mighty deliverance.

The name *Jabin* means "intelligent, observant; one who perceives; one with a natural mind." Jabin ruled over his kingdom—and the captive Israelites—from a town named *Hazor,* which means "enclosure."

As we have learned, the meanings of the names used in the Bible unlock many key truths to us. There is no more cruel bondage that exists over believers today than the bondage of those who choose to walk in disobedience to God, controlled by their intellect, their carnal mind, which is enmity against God. Such bondage to the carnal mind is the source of many forms of idolatry, witchcraft, and bondage.

Jabin's general was named *Sisera,* which means "meditational array," such as can be found in the carvings of idols (Judg. 4:2).

> And she sent and called Barak the son of Abinoam out of Kedeshnaphtali, and said unto him, Hath not the Lord God of Israel commanded, saying, Go and draw toward mount Tabor, and take with thee ten thousand men of the children of Naphtali and of the children of Zebulun? And I will draw unto thee to the river Kishon Sisera, the captain of Jabin's army, with his chariots and his multitude; and I will deliver him into thine hand.
>
> —Judges 4:6–7

> So God subdued on that day Jabin the king of Canaan before the children of Israel. And the hand of the children of Israel prospered, and prevailed against Jabin the king of Canaan, until they had destroyed Jabin king of Canaan.
>
> —verses 23–24

Jabin is another example of two biblical characters with the same name. Thus the spiritual picture we can glean from these two men's lives is particularly significant. This picture is one of the most graphic pictures of the victory of our forerunner Deborah and of the power of a believer over evil.

The first Jabin was a Canaanite king in the time of Joshua. His kingdom was centered in the city of Hazor. This first Jabin was defeated by *Joshua,* whose name means "savior." Joshua is the picture of Jesus Christ, who leads us into Canaan, empowers us to win over the enemy, and gives us the right to live for our inheritance. Jabin was totally defeated by Joshua and his seat of authority totally burned to the ground. Like Joshua's defeat of Jabin, Satan has been totally defeated by Jesus' atoning work at Calvary and by His descent into hell to defeat Satan's authority in the life of the believer. Christ took the keys of hell and death, and He burned Satan's seat of authority. Satan no longer has authority or control over us; Jesus took his authority and power and ascended to the Father in heaven.

> *Q: Describe the victory Jesus won for you from the power and captivity of Satan.*

_____

_____

_____

_____

Deborah's enemy, Jabin, from the same city of Hazor and a direct descendent of the first Jabin, could not rise again to attack Israel or keep it in captivity alone, so he made a league with Sisera (meaning "meditational array"), whose capital was Harosheth-Hagoyim ("fortress city of the nations"). This expanded understanding of the spiritual picture from the first Jabin is a picture of Satan's method of control over the body of Christ today. He makes a three-pronged league with the flesh—meditational array—and with the world—the city of many nations. Together, these three enemies of the people of God become one army encamped around the believer.

This army, comprised of the world, the flesh, and the devil, is controlling thousands of people today. So many people are bound in captivity, enduring the cruel, evil oppression of this army and awaiting the deliverance of the Deborahs and Baraks of today.

Jabin, along with his general Sisera, was a formidable foe.

> Now Heber the Kenite, which was of the children of Hobab the father in law of Moses, had severed himself from the Kenites, and pitched his tent unto the plain of Zaanaim, which is by Kedesh. And they shewed Sisera that Barak the son of Abinoam was gone up to mount Tabor. And Sisera gathered together all his chariots, even nine hundred chariots of iron, and all the people that were with him, from Harosheth of the Gentiles unto the river of Kishon.
>
> —JUDGES 4:11–13

Sisera came prepared to fight with a mighty host of men from the region between Harosheth and the river Kishon. It is believed that the name *Harosheth* means "forest." The name *Kishon,* although the name of a river, means "hard place." The Israelites were caught between a forest and a hard place! In addition, Sisera's army was equipped with nine hundred "chariots of iron." This indicates a chariot armed with iron scythes projecting from the axle on each side, by which infantry might be easily cut down or thrown into confusion.

Yet, through the deliverance of Deborah and Barak, Israel destroyed Hazor for the last time. It is never again mentioned in the Word. The armies of Jabin and

Sisera were totally defeated. When Jesus died for our sins, He defeated Satan for the last time. As we move into the characteristics of Deborah and Barak, we too will be able to lead many captives to a mighty deliverance.

> *Q: Have you ever faced a situation where you were bound in captivity between a forest (through which you could not see) and a hard place (through which you could not travel)? Describe this experience.*

_____

_____

_____

_____

> *Q: Describe the bondage you have endured from each of the following enemies.*

The world: _____

_____ .

The flesh: _____

_____ .

The devil: _____

_____ .

> *Q:* *Name at least three individuals who are bound to one of these enemies and under the cruel oppression of this three-pronged army.*

_____

_____

_____

> *Q:* *How can you help to lead these people to a mighty deliverance? Be specific.*

_____

_____

Though the devil has been ultimately defeated by the work of Christ, we are left to fight the ongoing scrimmages against the world, the flesh, and the devil—just as Deborah had to fight against this second Jabin.

When we understand that our oppressor has been defeated by Jesus long ago, we will conduct God's business right under the nose of our enemy. Deborah saw the oppression of this second Jabin. But she was also able to see a vision of victory as she remembered the defeat of the first Jabin long ago by Joshua. She would not succumb to this enemy. She would rise up with the supernatural assistance of Jehovah God and secure a final victory over the world, the flesh, and the devil. So can we! In the next chapter we will learn to do the same as we recognize our role as the mouthpiece for God.

5

Anointed As a
Mouthpiece for God

Deborah's spiritual authority as judge over Israel
had been established during a time of captivity.
But not only had God commissioned her as judge—
she was also divinely commissioned as prophetess.
Through her role as prophetess we can learn much
about how to have a spiritual impact on the lives of
others today, changing the course of history for them.

Deborah As a Prophetess

The name *prophetess* means "an inspired, anointed
female prophet of God." At this time of Deborah's
period in Israel, she had already been recognized as
prophetess—the anointed mouthpiece of God.

She was in a position of rulership before she assumed
the position of deliverer. Her rulership and authority had
been established by God—not because of anything she
did. It was established because of who she was in God.

A forerunner is not someone who is recognized

because he or she began a great revival. A forerunner is recognized because of his or her lifestyle,
his or her position in God—the revival comes as a
product of the lifestyle.

In Judges 4, verses 1–5 is an introduction to
Deborah, illustrating the right that Deborah had to
operate as a forerunner. Let's read those verses again:

> And the children of Israel again did evil in the
> sight of the LORD, when Ehud was dead. And
> the LORD sold them into the hand of Jabin king
> of Canaan, that reigned in Hazor; the captain of
> whose host was Sisera, which dwelt in Haro-
> sheth of the Gentiles. And the children of Israel
> cried unto the LORD: for he had nine hundred
> chariots of iron; and twenty years he mightily
> oppressed the children of Israel. And Deborah,
> a prophetess, the wife of Lapidoth, she judged
> Israel at that time. And she dwelt under the
> palm tree of Deborah between Ramah and
> Bethel in mount Ephraim: and the children of
> Israel came up to her for judgment.
>
> —JUDGES 4:1–5

Then verses 6–7 deal with the advanced operation
and characteristics of a forerunner.

> And she sent and called Barak the son of
> Abinoam out of Kedeshnaphtali, and said unto
> him, Hath not the LORD God of Israel com-
> manded, saying, Go and draw toward mount
> Tabor, and take with thee ten thousand men of
> the children of Naphtali and of the children of
> Zebulun? And I will draw unto thee to the river

Kishon Sisera, the captain of Jabin's army, with his chariots and his multitude; and I will deliver him into thine hand.

Here we see Deborah operating in the capacity of a mouthpiece for God—in her prophetic role.

Barak, who was a godly man, may have already been contemplating some great attempt to raise up an army and overcome the enemy forces of Jabin. But he had no army capable of defeating such an enemy. Perhaps he lacked the insight to know how to establish such an army.

But Deborah had received a clear word from God about this army. She reveals four significant facts about the army that would accompany Barak into battle against the enemy:

- The Lord had commanded that such an army be established.

Hath not the LORD God of Israel commanded...
—VERSE 6

Not only was it the right time for an army to be established—it was a command of God that it be done right now! No more delay, no more servitude, no more captivity—the fullness of time had come.

- The Lord commanded from where this army should be drawn.

Take...men of the children of Naphtali and of the children of Zebulun.
—VERSE 6

- The exact number of this army had been commanded by God.

  Take with thee ten thousand men...

  —VERSE 6

- The point of rendezvous for these ten thousand men had been established by God.

  Draw toward mount Tabor...

  —VERSE 6

Barak had perhaps also been inhibited from trying to made an offensive move against the enemy forces of Jabin and Sisera by a sense that he did not know how to engage the enemy in battle. Should he sneak into their camp under cover of darkness at night? Should he create a diversion to draw them from their fortified cities into battle? What exactly should he do?

Once again Deborah had been given a specific word for this specific occasion:

> I will draw unto thee to the river Kishon Sisera, the captain of Jabin's army, with his chariots and his multitude; and I will deliver him into thine hand.
>
> —VERSE 7

In the next chapter we will study the significance of these prophetic words from Deborah further. But it is important for us to understand at this point of our study that as the mouthpiece of God, Deborah was given very specific instructions for Barak.

Read again the specific instructions that were

given from God through Deborah to Barak. Then answer the following questions:

> *Q:* Describe a time when God gave you a specific action to take, gave you specific information about how to take this action, and told you what the specific outcome of this action would be.

_____

_____

_____

_____

_____

> *Q:* If you cannot recall an experience of specific revelation from God, write a prayer asking God to use you as a mouthpiece for Him by speaking in such a focused way into your spirit.

_____

_____

_____

_____

_____

As a forerunner, God may tell you something about another person who has stepped back into oppression of the world, the flesh, or the devil. He does not do this for you to take over that person's job and do it. Rather He speaks prophetically and specifically to you so that you may encourage that person in his weakness.

As a forerunner, you are called to encourage other believers in their divinely commissioned jobs, helping them to deal with the areas where they are afraid or confused. But if they refuse to do their job alone, you must be prepared to go along with them.

Kathryn Kuhlman's powerful healing ministry was characterized by her cry, "God, take not Your Holy Spirit from me." She could be heard agonizing during the preliminaries of her meetings that the Holy Spirit would be present to heal and do miracles. She knew the source of her anointing and power to bring healing to thousands.

Today we are in the fullness of time. I believe the coming of our Lord is nearer than we have ever dreamed it was. I don't know how long it is going to be before His coming, and I am not writing this study guide to predict it. But I believe something is about to happen. The spiritual winds that blow are whispering it; the church is praying for it. We are getting ready for something to explode. And God is getting both men and women ready to be a part of it. God doesn't operate by gender. He operates by anointing. He never said that *gender* breaks the yoke—He said the *anointing* destroys the yoke.

And it shall come to pass in that day, that his burden shall be taken away from off thy shoulder,

and his yoke from off thy neck, and the yoke
shall be destroyed because of the anointing.

—ISAIAH 10:27

God preserves those who have received an
anointing for service as His chosen vessels:

> Great deliverance giveth he to his king; and
> sheweth mercy to his anointed, to David, and
> to his seed for evermore.
>
> —PSALM 18:50

Now know I that the LORD saveth his anointed;
he will hear him from his holy heaven with the
saving strength of his right hand. Some trust in
chariots, and some in horses: but we will
remember the name of the LORD our God. They
are brought down and fallen: but we are risen,
and stand upright.

—PSALM 20:6–8

I have found David my servant; with my holy
oil have I anointed him: with whom my hand
shall be established: mine arm also shall
strengthen him. The enemy shall not exact
upon him; nor the son of wickedness afflict
him. And I will beat down his foes before his
face, and plague them that hate him. But my
faithfulness and my mercy shall be with him:
and in my name shall his horn be exalted.

—PSALM 89:20–24

> Q: *How has the anointing of God upon your life preserved you? Describe a specific time when the anointing broke a yoke that had bound you.*

_____

_____

_____

_____

_____

6

Called to Teamwork

Women of God, God has not placed us in an "It's us or them!" relationship with the men of God. We have been called to *teamwork*. Nowhere in the Word of God is this demonstrated more powerfully than in the story of Deborah and Barak's delivering victory over Jabin and Sisera.

Matthew Henry makes a very significant observation about the partnership of Deborah and Barak:

> Barak could do nothing without his head, nor she without his hands; but both together made a complete deliverer, and effected a complete deliverance.*

This can be a powerful revelation to the Christian woman of today who desires to be a forerunner to women who shall come after her. Note that the

The Bethany Parallel Commentary (Minneapolis, MN: Bethany House Publishers, 1985), s.v. Judges 4:4–9.

commentator did not say that Deborah and Barak made a "good partnership," or even that they made a "good team." He did not say that they were "the two deliverers who brought victory to Israel." He stated, "...both together made a complete deliverer."

One completed the other. One provided what the other needed. What an example of the partnership we are to have with men of God today.

> *Q: Have you, or others with whom you were in fellowship, ever felt inhibited from entering into a partnership of ministry with a person of the opposite gender? Describe your feelings.*

> *Q: How has God used you in partnership with a person of the opposite gender to accomplish a work for God?*

In the sixth verse of Judges 4, Barak emerges as the God-ordained partner to Deborah in this mighty deliverance of the Israelites.

As we begin to look at the life of Barak, we will take a look at the significance of his name. *Barak* means "lightning." Many times in the Old Testament, God's presence is manifested through lightning, thunder, and the noise of resounding trumpets. The name of Barak's father, *Abinoam,* means "the father is pleasantness." The place where Barak is told to assemble his army, *Mount Tabor,* means "purity." As we noted in an earlier chapter, Barak is going to battle against the second *Jabin,* who, together with the first Jabin, symbolizes the world, the flesh, and the devil.

Barak's name is seen to be synonymous with both the acts and the nature of God. Barak is birthed in the sacred place, nurtured in the knowledge that the Father is pleasantness, and taken to the mountain of purity to do battle against the world, the flesh, and the devil.

Jesus said that He gave us the Holy Spirit to teach us all truth, to separate us into righteousness by the convicting of sin. We are birthed in the sacred place in the union of the Holy Spirit and Jesus. As we grow in Jesus, He sends the Holy Spirit to nurture us in the nature and character of the Father (pleasantness). He brings us to a point of purity in Him to effectively do battle against the world, the flesh, and the devil. The name by which we are called— *Christian*—means "Christlike."

> ☑ *Look at the list below. Place a checkmark by the following characteristics of a Barak that you believe to be evident in your life.*

☐ *An understanding of God's truth*

☐ *Separation from the world unto righteousness*

☐ *A greater evidence of your birth into Jesus Christ*

☐ *A greater evidence of your birth into the Holy Spirit*

☐ *Nurturing in the pleasant nature and character of the Father*

☐ *Evidence of purity in your life*

☐ *Preparation to do battle with the world, the flesh, and the devil*

> *Q: Which of the above characteristics of a Barak need to become more dominant in your life?*

_____

_____

And Deborah arose, and went with Barak to Kedesh.

—JUDGES 4:9

Kedesh was the home of the Gershonite Levites, whose sole responsibility was to move the structure of the tabernacle as God commanded. Our responsibility is to move the structure of the tabernacle (our bodies) because He lives in us. Wherever we go, the tabernacle must be set up as a safe haven to those around us.

Barak took ten thousand men from the tribes of Zebulun and Naphtali. Zebulun was a tribe of writers and lawyers (cf. Judges 5 and 6). Naphtali was a tribe located around the Sea of Galilee, a tribe of fisherman (Matt. 4:13). From these two tribes we get a revelation of the gospel (fishermen) and the Law (writers and lawyers), together conquering the enemy.

In his blessing to the children of Israel, Moses blessed both tribes.

> And of Zebulun he said, Rejoice, Zebulun, in thy going out....They shall call the people unto the mountain; there they shall offer sacrifices of righteousness: for they shall suck of the abundance of the seas, and of treasures hid in the sand.
>
> —DEUTERONOMY 33:18–19

> And of Naphtali he said, O Naphtali, satisfied with favour, and full with the blessing of the LORD: possess thou the west and the south.
>
> —VERSE 23

This is a beautiful picture of the victory Deborah and Barak would achieve with the help of the tribes of Zebulun and Naphtali.

Let's take an even closer look at these two tribes. Zebulun was Leah's last son. His name means "dwelling," because she said, "Now will my husband dwell with me" (Gen. 30:20). From him we see a picture of the bride dwelling with the groom. Leah has finally rested in the safety of the love of her groom. As forerunners, we need to have security in the knowledge that we can rest in the love of our Groom, which is not earned, but is one of our benefits.

Naphtali was the last son conceived of Rachel's maid Bilhah (Gen. 30:7). His name meant "wrestling," for she said, "With great wrestlings have I wrestled with my sister, and I have prevailed" (Gen. 30:8). This is a reference to the competitive spirit between Rachel and Leah to bear sons for Jacob.

In his letter to the church in Rome, Paul compares Leah and Rachel. Leah is seen as the life of the Law; Rachel represents the life of Calvary. The life of Calvary wrestles and wins over the Law, grace backs the Law, and the two together overcome the enemy, the world, the flesh, and the devil. (See Romans 8.)

> *Q: Do you have a security in the love of your Groom, the Lord Jesus Christ? How has His love made you secure?*

Q: Within your spiritual life have you recognized the power of the Law and God's grace working together to give you victory over the enemy? How can you define this partnership of Law and grace?

_____

_____

_____

_____

_____

_____

The partnership of Deborah and Barak was cemented as Barak spoke these words:

> If thou wilt go with me, then I will go: but if thou wilt not go with me, then I will not go.
> —JUDGES 4:8

The Septuagint made a remarkable addition to the speech of Barak: "If thou wilt go with me I will go; but if thou wilt not go with me I will not go; because I know not the day in which the Lord will send his angel to give me success." By which he appears to mean that, although he was certain of a divine call to this work, yet, as he knew not the time in which it would be proper for him to make the attack, he wished that Deborah, on whom the Divine

Spirit constantly rested, would accompany him
to let him know when to strike that blow,
which he knew would be decisive.*

With Deborah's presence with him, Barak went
down from Mount Tabor in full confidence. Assured
of victory by the prophetic words of Deborah, the
army of Israel relinquished their position of advantage on the hill and rushed into the plain in the path
of the iron chariots they feared.

What a dynamic duo for God! This is the pattern
of partnership to which God is calling men and
women today. Such teamwork will bring a mighty
victory over the enemies that threaten to oppress the
people of God.

---

* *The Bethany Parallel Commentary*, see the comment at Judges 4:8 by Adam Clarke.

7

A Divine Mandate

It is clear from Deborah's success as a leader over the nation of Israel—even while it was bound in captivity to the enemy—that her authority had been established by God. She was not given this position because of what she had accomplished politically for the nation. She was God's appointed leader over Israel for that time. She had received a divine mandate—an assigned task that was divinely predestined.

Deborah was living in a time when the people of Israel were suffering the consequences of their own disobedience before God. There was a great vacuum of the presence of God in the land. Deborah had been called to become the spokeswoman for God— a forthtelling of divine revelation that would lead the nation to victory.

The Bible gives us many examples of women who have been given a divine mandate in the midst of a great vacuum of the presence of God to become spokeswomen for God. We have mentioned some of these in an earlier chapter. There was Esther, who was brought to the kingdom "for such a time as this." Ruth was mandated to be a part of the lineage of Christ.

In the New Testament we have the record of another spokeswoman for God. In the fourth chapter of John, we see God choose a most unlikely candidate to become a voice for Him. Born in a country that was openly hostile to the people of God, a nation that worshiped false gods, this woman was even an outcast from her own people because of her disobedient and evil lifestyle. Yet one day she met the Son of God at a well in Samaria, and her life was transformed. As the Messiah, the Christ, entered her life, she received a divine mandate that caused her to run back to her city, where she told the entire city the good news of the gospel—leading them into a great spiritual victory.

Read the story of the woman at the well of Samaria from John 4:5–30. Consult a Bible dictionary for a brief history of the Samaritan people. Then answer the following questions:

> *Q: How did the Samaritan nation at the time of the story of the woman at the well compare in lifestyle to the nation of Israel at the time of Deborah's rulership?*

Q: In the brief record in John 4 of the Samaritan woman's response to Christ and her willingness to speak for Christ to her city, what godly characteristics can you detect in her life that were also present in the life of Deborah?

_____
_____
_____
_____
_____
_____
_____

Q: What is the evidence of a divine mandate upon the Samaritan woman's life?

_____
_____
_____
_____
_____
_____

> *Q: What spiritual parallels can you see between the victory of Deborah and Barak over Jabin and the success of the Samaritan woman in bringing her entire city to Christ (John 4:30)?*

_____

_____

_____

_____

Women of God today also are positioned to be divinely mandated as spokeswomen for God. Many spiritual parallels are easily recognizable between our cities, our communities, our nation, and those of Deborah and the woman at the well of Samaria. This is the appointed time. This is the time for liberation and the cessation of bondage for the people around us. But we must recognize God's mandate to us to become His spokeswomen.

In my book *The Next Move of God,* I prophesied of a great move of God that would bring forth resurrection life like a flood, which would run to those "in mountains, and in dens and caves of the earth" (Heb. 11:38). This is the great victory I described:

> Our government, our church denominations, our social organizations, our school systems, our industries—which have become corrupt, motivated by self-promotion, serving for gold and silver and ruled by covetous practices—will all be changed by the power of God's divine

presence. This move of God will be so powerful that throughout our land we will see a return to the great historical foundations of this nation, which declares that in God we trust.*

This great victory is being brought forth in the divine mandate of men and women who, like Deborah, are willing to become the spokesmen and spokeswomen for God.

> *Q:* Think about your neighborhood, community, and city. How are the people you know like the captive nations of Israel and Samaria that we have discussed?

_____

_____

_____

> *Q:* How can you be a "Deborah," speaking forth the counsel of God to effect a great victory in your community?

_____

_____

_____

* Fuchsia Pickett, *The Next Move of God* (Lake Mary, FL: Creation House, 1994).

> *Q: Write a prayer asking God to help you recognize His divine mandate to speak forth His counsel in your community.*

_____

_____

_____

Unfortunately, some women in ministry have left bad tracks with which others have to deal. Their haughtiness and willingness to fight and argue their opinions or defend their calling have turned many men off to the messenger as well as the message. We do not need to defend the anointing—it speaks for itself.

When Deborah called Barak before her to deliver the counsel of God, she did not rebuke him for his inaction up to that time. In love she questioned him first:

> And she sent and called Barak the son of Abinoam out of Kedeshnaphtali, and said unto him, Hath not the LORD God of Israel commanded, saying, Go and draw toward mount Tabor, and take with thee ten thousand men of the children of Naphtali and of the children of Zebulun?
>
> —JUDGES 4:6

But Barak seemed reluctant to lead his army into victory, resisting her counsel and expressing his timidity to confront the task alone. Yet even then, when Deborah had to rebuke his unwillingness to move forward as the Lord commanded, still she assured him that he had her support:

> Barak said unto her, If thou wilt go with me, then I will go: but if thou wilt not go with me, then I will not go. And she said, I will surely go with thee: notwithstanding the journey that thou takest shall not be for thine honour; for the LORD shall sell Sisera into the hand of a woman. And Deborah arose, and went with Barak to Kedesh.
> —VERSES 8–9

As spokeswomen and forerunners, we must never deal with those God causes us to deal with in anger. We must never be haughty and judgmental. Even when we must rebuke their inactivity, we must be willing to nurture them.

Deborah was attempting to get Barak to recognize the counsel God had already given to him about the circumstances and the outcome of the battle. God had already told him who the enemy was, where the battle was to be fought, and the tools of warfare he was to use (tribes of Naphtali and Zebulun). God had even stated that He would bring the enemy out to Barak. Yet still Barak would not obey.

As a result of her questioning Barak with the right spirit, Deborah showed Barak the truth of his communication with God. She was able to expose the fear he had because he did not know when the battle was to begin.

As spokeswomen, we are to gently expose the area by which Satan has bound those to whom God sends us. God has identified the enemy of our soul. He has identified the place where the battle is to be fought. He has identified the tools we are to use. He has warned us that periodically He will allow Satan to wage a battle with us, but He promises that by following His counsel we will win. But just as He did with Barak, He never reveals the time or day the battle will begin.

Think about the circumstances of your life. Are you facing the oppression of the enemy? Describe this oppression by answering the following questions.

> *Q: What is the area of your life that is experiencing the oppression of the enemy?*

_____

_____

_____

_____

_____

> *Q: What tools has the Lord revealed to you that you are to use to overcome the enemy?*

_____

_____

_____

_____

_____

Q: Write a prayer asking God to go with you into battle, giving you a clear mandate that will achieve a mighty victory over this area of oppression.

_____

_____

_____

_____

_____

_____

8

A Directed Message

Deborah was able to fulfill the divine mandate that God had given to her because she had learned how to listen to the voice of God. She had heard God's directed message, given to her at a specific point of time for a specific course of action. Perhaps this is the greatest distinguishing factor between her and Barak. Although a godly man, Barak was unable to figure out how to make an aggressive stand against the enemy because he had not received revelation from God.

Jesus states the need to hear God's directed message:

> But blessed are your eyes, for they see: and your ears, for they hear. For verily I say unto you, That many prophets and righteous men have desired to see those things which ye see, and have not seen them; and to hear those things which ye hear, and have not heard them.
> —MATTHEW 13:16–17

I'm sure that at some time you have tried to communicate an important message to another person and felt that although the person heard your words, he or she did not understand your message. Perhaps you have spoken earnestly to a friend and, by your friend's response, realized that she did not hear your heart although perhaps she heard your words. Instead she interpreted what you said according to her own preconceived attitude, perspective, prejudice, or emotional response.

> *Q: Describe such an experience, relating how you knew she had not heard the intent of your heart.*

_____

_____

_____

Many times in the Word of God the phrase "he that hath ears to hear, let him hear" is used (Matt. 11:15). The Greek word for *hear* used in this phrase is *akouo,* which means to hear in a natural sense with the ears and to understand the words that are spoken. Jesus used the same word when He spoke of what He had heard from the Father:

> I have many things to say and to judge of you: but he that sent me is true; and I speak to the world those things which I have heard of him.
> —JOHN 8:26

Jesus' words refer to the intimate relationship He enjoyed with His Father, communing with Him while He was here on earth. God wants those who speak for Him on earth today to have the same kind of relationship with Him, hearing and understanding His heart in the words He has given us. In order to do so, we must follow these important steps:

1. *Cultivate quietness.*

> Be still, and know that I am God.
> —PSALM 46:10

Quietness does not come naturally to most of us. This is true to such an extent that we often ask someone who is not overly talkative, "Is something wrong?"

We wake up in the morning to the automatic sounds of our clock/radios...we drive to and from work listening to our tapes and car radios...we walk or jog with our portable radios plugged into our ears...we even fall asleep to the sounds coming from a CD or tape. No longer do we hear the natural sounds of the birds, and the water lapping against the shore goes unnoticed. It is almost as if there is a fear of silence in our culture today.

There is more to quietness than an absence of external noise. There is a cessation of our frantic thoughts and pursuits, our insatiable desires, and selfish motivations. As we cultivate that kind of quietness, God's directed message will become a reality in our hearts—not just in our ears.

Q: *How do you cultivate quietness within your own spiritual life?*

_____

_____

_____

_____

_____

_____

_____

_____

2. *Meditate on the Word.*

> Blessed is the man that walketh not in the counsel of the ungodly, nor standeth in the way of sinners, nor sitteth in the seat of the scornful. But his delight is in the law of the LORD; and in his law doth he meditate day and night.
>
> —PSALM 1:1–2

Meditating on the Scriptures will help us to understand the way God thinks, His principles, and His attitude toward sin as well as His love for the sinner. We will become familiar with God's vocabulary. We will learn to distinguish His voice from the voice of the accuser. His directed message will be clearly distinguishable.

> *Q: Describe a time when meditating on the Scriptures helped you to clearly discern a message God wanted you to know concerning a specific situation in your life or in the life of another.*

_____

_____

_____

_____

_____

_____

_____

3. *Ask God questions.*

> Then the LORD answered Job out of the whirlwind.
> —JOB 38:1

Many times as I have meditated on the Word and asked God about something I did not understand, He would begin to give me understanding through another verse that shed light on the one I was questioning, or He otherwise opened my understanding to the truth He was revealing. God welcomes our questions and is there to answer them for us. It is the Holy Spirit's task to lead us into all truth (John 16:13).

Q: What are three questions for which you would like to receive an answer from God right now?

_____

_____

_____

_____

_____

_____

_____

_____

4. *Anticipate hearing God speak.*

> Unto thee will I cry, O LORD my rock; be not silent to me.
>
> —PSALM 28:1

From the creation of mankind in the Garden of Eden, God has desired to commune with His people. The Spirit-filled believer has the greatest potential for hearing God's voice, because God dwells in our hearts by His Holy Spirit. As we quiet our minds and open our hearts to His Word, we can anticipate hearing the voice of God communing with us, Spirit to spirit. He will give us many directed messages for ourselves and for others who will listen.

*Q: Name a situation for which you are antici-
pating an answer from God.*

_____

_____

_____

_____

5. *Respond to what you hear.*

But prove yourselves doers of the word, and
not merely hearers who delude themselves.
—JAMES 1:22, NAS

After we have heard God, it is imperative that we
obey what He has said. This was the problem with
Barak—although God had directed him to make a
stand against Jabin and Sisera, he had not yet
responded when Deborah called him to her.

*Q: Have you ever disobeyed a word that God
gave to you? What was the result?*

_____

_____

_____

_____

6. *Look for confirmation.*

> Every matter must be established [confirmed]
> by the testimony of two or three witnesses.
> —2 Corinthians 13:1, NIV

Even sincere believers have erred in their interpretation of the Scriptures and have preached the error as truth, bringing harm to the body of Christ. It is vital to confirm the directed message we have received from God with other men and women of God who can confirm or correct our "revelations."

> *Q: Name two or three men and women of God to whom you have gone for a confirmation of the directed message God had given to you.*

_____

_____

_____

_____

If we follow these six principles for hearing the voice of God, our lives will be transformed by His presence and by His directed messages into our life and, through us, into the lives of others.*

Deborah had received a directed message from God. This message:

---
* These six principles have been adapted from chapter four of my book, *Receiving Divine Revelation.*

- Came from the sound of a clear voice.
- Contained a clear word from God.
- Gave a clear command—with directions and counsel.
- Ended with a clear promise—"I will draw them to the river."

Because Deborah had received this directed message, she was able to give good counsel to Barak: "The LORD God of Israel has commanded you and said to you…" God had spoken, and Barak would have to obey or disobey on that basis.

9

A Declared Motive

Deborah's life reflected her motivation for all that she did—she loved the people of Israel and desired their deliverance from the enemy. She wanted to see God's people set free; she wanted them to bring home the spoil of the enemy. She wasn't going out to make a name for herself or to build her own reputation as a mighty minister of God. She had been sitting under a palm tree ministering for twenty years. Now the moment had come for which God had predestined her. She was instrumental in bringing forty years of peace to Israel, ending their suffering of twenty years of captivity.

It was not Deborah's intention to lord it over Barak; she was not being self-assertive or aggressive. She did not sit in a place of competition with men or usurp the place of a man. Barak confirms this fact by saying to her, "If thou wilt go with me, then I will go; but if thou wilt not go with me, then I will not go" (Judg. 4:8). His confidence in her word evoked

immediate obedience. And his confidence in her
person desired her presence with him, knowing that
God was with her. Perhaps he felt he would need
her counsel and further direction from the Lord in
the ensuing battle.

Deborah consented to go; she declared that "now
is the time for action." She declared to Barak that
God had already delivered Sisera into his hand. The
Lord threw the enemy into panic.

Women are being called, brought to the kingdom
in a greater way than ever—for such a time as this.

I don't know of anything on earth any greater and
more humbling than to know that God brought you
here at *this* time—He could have waited for some
other time. But He brought you to the kingdom *for
such an hour as this.*

> *Q: Has God placed a mandate on your life and
> given you a directed message "for such an
> hour as this"? Describe your message and
> the sense of urgency you feel to declare this
> message.*

_____

_____

_____

_____

_____

God is raising up Deborahs, women who will become His spokeswomen, forerunners for future women of God. He is not raising you up for dictatorship...He does not want you to aggressively proclaim your message as you attempt to stifle the message of a man to whom God has breathed a directed message also.

God doesn't want you to be a man...or to attempt to take a man's place in ministry. He does not want you to view your role as a competitor to men in ministry.

God is calling to a partnership of ministry with men. Like Deborah and Barak, God needs your teamwork.

> ✔ *Place a checkmark beside the erroneous ways in which you have observed women attempt to move forward into ministry:*

☐ *By attempting to establish a spiritual "dictatorship" ministry*

☐ *By aggressively proclaiming her message while denigrating the message of a man in ministry*

☐ *By attempting to adopt the characteristics of a man in ministry or by attempting to usurp the authority of male leadership*

☐ *By trying to compete with male leadership*

> *Q: What have been the results of the above types of female leadership?*

_____

_____

_____

_____

_____

_____

God is changing much of the church world—tearing down the tradition and prejudices that have hindered the partnership of men and women in ministry. When I began ministry, there was no Women Aglow organization. There were no women taking part in leadership seminars. There were very few husband-and-wife partnership teams.

But today God is beginning to unravel all the prejudice, customs, and traditions to motivate men and women to partnership in ministry according to the principles of Galatians 3:26–28:

> For ye are all the children of God by faith in Christ Jesus. For as many of you as have been baptized into Christ have put on Christ. There is neither Jew nor Greek, there is neither bond nor free, there is neither male nor female: for ye are all one in Christ Jesus.

This is the declared motive of the Deborahs and Baraks of today. The hindrances of traditions, denominationalism, prejudices, culture, and customs are being destroyed as we partner in ministry and declare to one another: "We won't go without you!"

> *Q: Write your own declaration of motivation, promising to partner together with others regardless of gender or any other perceived differences in order to win a mighty victory over the Jabins and Siseras who hold the world captive to their oppression.*

_____

_____

_____

_____

10

The Other Face of Faith

God is glorified when He finds Deborahs and Baraks who are willing to walk together in unity against the enemy. When Paul declared God's call to unity in Galatians 3:28, he prefaced his declaration with the statement: "But after that faith is come..." (Gal. 3:25). Only as faith comes to our hearts, removing us from the tutorship of the Law, will we walk in liberty from the prejudice of class distinction and gender. Faith is coming to the church, and truth is being restored.

Let me be quick to add that I am not advocating an adherence to the women's lib philosophy—I don't believe in it. It was born out of rebellion. I am not a *feminist;* I am *feminine.*

> *Q:* *What observations have you made of the women's lib and feminist movements that substantiate the claim that such movements were "born out of rebellion"?*

_____

_____

_____

_____

> *Q:* *What do you believe to be some of the results of such philosophies?*

_____

_____

_____

_____

It is true that man is head of the home, and that involves more than just being boss. It is not an issue of authority, but of God's predestined plan—one that is being unfolded in the earth today.

We are living in an hour that was prophesied on the day of Pentecost almost two thousand years ago. Peter declared:

> And it shall come to pass in the last days, saith God, I will pour out of my Spirit upon all flesh: and your sons and your daughters shall prophesy,

and your young men shall see visions, and your
old men shall dream dreams: And on my servants
and on my handmaidens I will pour out in those
days of my Spirit; and they shall prophesy.

—ACTS 2:17–18

A more accurate translation is "the last of the last
days." As we observe the church today, we see that
God is raising up men and women together and
pouring out His Spirit upon them to prophesy. We are
already seeing the glory of God burst forth as revival
is breaking loose. As men and women move together
in God, a mighty victory over the oppression of the
enemy is taking place. And this time, we won't just go
after the spoils, but after the head of the enemy,
because "Deborah" and "Barak" are going together.

> Q: Briefly describe the breaking loose of
> revival that you may have observed as a
> result of a partnership ministry between a
> Deborah and a Barak.

_____

_____

_____

_____

_____

_____

> *Q: Give the names and ministry focuses for three Deborah and Barak teams of which you are aware.*

_____

_____

_____

_____

_____

_____

_____

Not everyone within the church is willing to work in partnership with one another to achieve victory over the enemy. The Holy Spirit has impressed upon me that there are at least five hindering concepts that must be destroyed before unity can truly be achieved.*

Let's take a brief look at some of these:

Prejudice

Unreasonable biases, judgments, or opinions, held in disregard of facts, breed suspicion, intolerance, or hatred; they have no place in Christ's church. Whether it is against race, gender, sect, class, or status, prejudice will keep us from hearing and receiving the truth of God as revealed by the Holy Spirit.

---

* The material on these hindering concepts has been adapted from chapter eight of my book, *The Next Move of God.*

Paul admonished Timothy:

> ...guard and keep [these rules] without personal prejudice or favor, doing nothing from partiality.
> —1 TIMOTHY 5:21, AMP

Paul teaches us to live in an attitude of humility, esteeming one another above ourselves, loving one another fervently, and looking out for the interests of others.

> *Q:* *What personal prejudices, biases, judgments, or opinions do you still need the Holy Spirit to assist you in overcoming?*

_____

_____

_____

_____

_____

Denominationalism

A denomination is a class or society of individuals supporting a system of principles and called by the same name. As long as a denomination remains open to the life of Jesus, it is not harmful. However, when denominational doctrines are taught with dogmatic finality, greater streams of truth that would flow through it are limited.

Elitism, legalism, and judgmental attitudes almost

always result from such dogma. Such denomination-alism obscures the directed message that God wants the church to hear today.

> *Q: How has the dogma of the denomination to which you belong helped or hindered people hearing the directed message of God?*

_____

_____

_____

_____

_____

_____

_____

Human tradition

Webster's dictionary defines *tradition* as "an inherited, established, or customary pattern of thought, action, or behavior; the handing down of information, beliefs, and customs by word of mouth or by example from one generation to another without written instructions."

The Pharisees were often guilty of hindering the message Christ wanted to make known by their confrontations of human tradition. Peter reminds us that we "were not redeemed with perishable things like silver and gold from your futile way of life inherited from your forefathers" (1 Pet. 1:18, NAS). Today, God is creating in the hearts of His people a new hunger and thirst for His Word that supersedes the traditions of man.

> *Q: What human traditions have hindered you from understanding the revelations of God? How did you overcome these traditions?*

_____

_____

_____

_____

_____

Culture

Perhaps nothing is more basic to our natural thinking than culture—the concepts, habits, arts, institutions, and refinements of thought, manners, and taste that characterize our native environment. We must be delivered from our bondage to culture in order to allow Christ to move in us and through us to any culture. He brings a new and higher way of life that transcends the limitations of culture.

As we learn to embrace a lifestyle without compromise with the external, we will be able to live a godly life in our sinful cultures. We can learn to live *in* this world without being part of it. Then we will be salt and light to those around us.

> *Q:* *What cultural habits have you observed that sometimes are stumbling blocks to the forth-telling of God's message to those of another culture?*

_____

_____

_____

_____

_____

Today's spokeswomen and spokesmen must have moved to the "other face of faith." It is faith that removes these hindering barriers to unity and partnership among people in God's church. Desire the "other face of faith."

11

Restored to Service

A s we move to the "other face of faith," God will be able to restore the church to its rightful place of leadership and service in the world today. As Barak stepped forward in faith with Deborah, God was able to remove his hindering fear, and together they reached great victory. So can the church today.

The Book of Genesis declares:

> And God said, Let us make man in our image, after our likeness.
>
> —GENESIS 1:26

The image of God is revealed in God the Father, God the Son, and God the Holy Spirit. Each member of the Godhead has a unique and distinct role and function. Mankind was made in "their" likeness—a plural term that incorporates the characteristics of each member of the Godhead.

When God used the word *man* (*anthropos*) in the Book of Genesis, He did not refer to the masculine gender—He referred to *mankind*. That means that mankind—male *and* female—is created in the image of God. God took His threefold image and made mankind in one created form.

God ordained that it would take both male and female to reveal the image of God. I believe it is time for the world to see the other "face" of God. Though God is neither male nor female, He wants to express His image through mankind, requiring both genders to work together in order to express the Father's image. The threefold image of God—that of the Father, the Son, and the Holy Spirit—is only fully expressed in man and woman together.

> *Q: Beside each of the following characteristics of the Godhead, write down one way that characteristic can be expressed by a man and one way that characteristic can be expressed by a woman.*

*Creator:*_____

_____.

*All-powerful:*_____

_____.

*All-knowing:*_____

_____.

*Present everywhere:*_____

_____.

Q: Think about some of the other characteristics of the Godhead. Can you think of a characteristic that is uniquely better expressed through the female gender? Through the male gender?

_____

_____

_____

_____

When God made Adam and Eve, He did not position one to rule over the other—either man over woman or woman over man. He intended for them to walk side by side as the glory of His presence enveloped both of them. God walked with them in the garden and revealed Himself to both man and woman. He wanted to walk with both of them.

God never intended for His presence to be locked into a tabernacle behind a veil. But that was the only way He could come to man after man fell and sin entered the world. Christ's victory over man's sin rent the veil and ushered in the presence of God in a new way. God's original intent was for our inner man to be a sanctuary into which He could pour His presence—His wisdom, His righteousness, His holiness. With Christ's victory over sin, God poured His wisdom, righteousness, and holiness into the sanctuaries of the hearts of mankind—man and woman. God is bringing the church—men and women—into unity in order to reveal Himself to the world.

> Q: *Think about your own life since the Holy Spirit moved into your "sanctuary." Give an example of the way God has poured each of the following three characteristics into your life.*

His wisdom: _____.

His righteousness: _____.

His holiness: _____.

Which of these characteristics do you need the most?

_____

As we look back to the disobedience of Adam and Eve, we see that God decreed to the woman:

> ...and thy desire shall be to thy husband, and he shall rule over thee.
> —GENESIS 3:16

The Hebrew is better translated "because of the turning of your heart to your husband [from God, implied], he shall rule over thee." Many have misunderstood this to be a *command* of God that man is to rule over the woman. This has become one of the dogmas of church doctrine.

I believe such a dogma to be the doctrine of fallen man. The "turning of your heart to your husband" was actually a *consequence* of the woman's turning to man and away from God at the moment of her disobedient act. This is an illustration of the false doctrines within the church that must be cleansed from our hearts.

The more restoration men and women enjoy, the less ruling over each other there is. The husband becomes the protector, provider, comforter, and leader, laying down his life as the Scriptures teach (Eph. 5:25). The wife has turned her heart back to God and is free to obey Him in building the kingdom of God with her husband. God intended for the husband and wife to be leaders together, having dominion over the earth.

> *Q: How can this understanding of the consequence of sin help to build the foundation for a strong partnership in ministry between male and female leaders?*

> *Q: How can it strengthen the bond of love and commitment in a marriage relationship?*

As long as we try to live our lives under the limitations of the Law, we will have a different message. But when faith is come, it breaks down the Law. Whose law was it that women couldn't prophesy? Whose law was it that women couldn't pastor? Whose law was it that said women couldn't hear from God? It was man's law.

The disciples would not have known that Jesus had been resurrected if it had not been for a woman. The disciples were not at the tomb first—a woman was. During the time Jesus ministered on earth, only two people were mentioned in God's Word for having divine revelation regarding His life and ministry. One of them was Peter, who was given a glimpse of revelation and who subsequently declared who Jesus was. The other was the woman who broke her alabaster box on His feet and anointed Him for His death, burial, and resurrection. Until Mary's anointing of Jesus, the disciples had not understood that Jesus was going to die. They thought that He was going to set up an earthly kingdom.

Several times Jesus rebuked His disciples, saying "You don't understand." But this woman came to worship and love Him as a result of her divine revelation. She broke her alabaster box of precious ointment over Him, pouring it upon His head and feet. In response He told His disciples and the others who observed her act of ministry that she had anointed Him for His death. This same woman was the first one at the tomb.

Q: Give an example to show how a Peter in ministry today may have declared the Messiahship of Christ to those who needed to hear the liberating message.

Q: What Mary do you know who has proclaimed by her act of anointing that Christ's death and resurrection power are available to the world?

Just as the believers in Peter's day needed His declaration of Christ as Messiah, so too today we need the Peters who will declare the revelation of Christ the Messiah who can conquer their sin and oppression. Just as the disciples and others needed Mary's declaration of Jesus as the anointed Messiah being prepared for His sacrificial death and resurrection victory over death and sin, so the world needs Marys who will reveal Christ's resurrection power to set it free.

Today we have been redeemed to live under faith—not under Law. We have been restored to service. We have been liberated that we may liberate others. But to be effective, we must be unified as a mighty team that stands against the enemy's bondage. We must work together to set the captives free.

I can hardly believe I have lived to see the hour that God is raising up prophets and prophetesses and apostles and teachers, men and women who will be restored to the image of God and reveal Him to the world. As He does, we are going to see an old-fashioned, heaven-sent, gully-washing, sin-killing revival—and God is going to overdo and outdo everything the devil has ever done.

12

"Rise Up,
O Deborah!"

Because she trusted God fully, Deborah was able to lead Israel to victory. The ultimate result of Deborah's leadership was the end of captivity and suffering for Israel—and the beginning of forty years of peace.

I believe God is raising up "Deborahs" today. Women are being called into leadership in the kingdom in a greater way than ever before—"for such a time as this"!

Have you grasped the magnitude and wonder of God's plan for restoration for our individual lives and for His church as it is foreshadowed prophetically in the life of Deborah? Have you recognized God's call upon your life to become a spokeswoman, a forerunner for the women of today? Or has your mind defeated you with thoughts of *It's too good to be true* or *Maybe someday, but surely not now?*

> *Q: Describe the call you believe God has placed on your life.*

_____

_____

_____

_____

God gives us a mighty call to service in the Book of Isaiah:

> Arise, shine; for thy light is come, and the glory of the LORD is risen upon thee. For, behold, the darkness shall cover the earth, and gross darkness the people: but the LORD shall arise upon thee, and his glory shall be seen upon thee.
> —ISAIAH 60:1–2

As we look around at the wickedness and oppression in our world, we must conclude that our society today qualifies as a time when darkness covers the earth. The Jabins and Siseras have held many captive to the devil's oppressive captivity for many years. It is significant that Isaiah's exhortation to arise was written emphatically in the present tense.

Like Deborah's call to Barak to obey the word of God and move forward into battle, God's clarion call is calling for Deborahs to arise and work in partnership with others to effect a great victory over the enemy.

Do you desire to be a part of this mighty move of God within the church today? As the Deborahs and Baraks of today arise, the church is going to be restored to the inheritance that Christ died to give her. She will become a glorious church, without spot or wrinkle.

> *Q: What specific work would you like to accomplish for God?*

_____

_____

_____

The spoils of the enemy will become the inheritance of the church. When Joseph was reunited with his brothers in Egypt, he addressed the issue of their sin against him with these words:

> Ye thought evil against me; but God meant it unto good, to bring to pass, as it is this day, to save much people alive.
> —GENESIS 50:20

When the enemy destroyed everything Job possessed, except his very life, God "turned the captivity of Job" (Job 42:10).

> So the LORD blessed the latter end of Job more than his beginning...
> —JOB 42:12

In the Book of Psalms, God spoke prophetically of the end of Israel's captivity:

When the LORD turned again the captivity of Zion, we were like them that dream. Then was our mouth filled with laughter, and our tongue with singing: then said they among the heathen, The LORD hath done great things for them. The LORD hath done great things for us; whereof we are glad. Turn again our captivity, O LORD, as the streams in the south. They that sow in tears shall reap in joy. He that goeth forth and weepeth, bearing precious seed, shall doubtless come again with rejoicing, bringing his sheaves with him.

—PSALM 126

Therefore arise, O Deborah! Become a forerunner for women of God. Recognize your mandate to be an anointed spokeswoman for God in your world today. Team with your Barak to win an eternal victory over the enemy. Allow God to restore you—and those to whom He sends you—into His divine inheritance of rejoicing and joy.

> *Q: How has this study on Deborah enlightened your understanding of God's purposes in your own life?*

89

If you enjoyed Deborah, **here are some other SpiritLed Woman Study Guides from Charisma House that we think will minister to you...**

Esther
Fuchsia Pickett
ISBN: 0-88419-584-8
Retail Price: $6.99

Esther is a prophetic message revealed to the "church within the church." Through allegory and type, you will explore deep truths concerning your relationship with God, both as an individual and corporately, and His plan for the church.

Ruth
Fuchsia Pickett
ISBN: 0-88419-585-6
Retail Price: $6.99

This allegorical account of the Book of Ruth illuminates this historical love story, pivotal in the genealogy of the house of David and of Jesus Christ. You will explore the deep truths concerning our relationship with God individually and corporately.

How to Search the Scriptures
Fuchsia Pickett
ISBN: 0-88419-587-2
Retail Price: $12.99

This study book will teach you the necessity of constant and faithful study of the Bible. By doing so, you will be able to apply its teachings to your own spiritual life and use the Word in your ministry to others. This study not only teaches you how to study and interpret God's Word. It outlines several methods of Bible study, including the synthetic and inductive methods of study and studying by topics, types or biographies.

 To pick up a copy of any of these titles, contact your local Christian bookstore or order online at www.charismawarehouse.com.